Under His Wings

Bonnie Inkster

SM**5**TH
S T O R E S

Kelowna, BC

Canada

ISBN: 095633427X
ISBN-13: 978-0-9563342-7-5

DEDICATION

To my loving husband who always encourages and blesses
me. He is my best friend who continually calls forth my
potential.

CONTENTS

ACKNOWLEDGMENTS

Scriptures taken from the Holy Bible, New International Version®, NIV®. Copyright © 1973, 1978, 1984, 2011 by Biblica, Inc.™ Used by permission of Zondervan. All rights reserved worldwide. www.zondervan.com The "NIV" and "New International Version" are trademarks registered in the United States Patent and Trademark Office by Biblica, Inc.™

Bonnie Inkster

1 INTRODUCTION

Psalm 91 is a wonderful description of the fatherhood of God and His love for us. Jesus said that as believers we live in the world but are not of it. This means that we face many storms and obstacles in life as does all mankind but...But we have a heavenly father that we can draw into during these times.

As a father He covers us, shelters us, protects us and blesses us. All we need to do is turn our faces towards Him and call on Him. He delights to respond to His children.

Under His Wings is a devotional that powerfully extrapolates each verse into a fullness of meaning using references to other portions of scripture to illustrate all that it is meant to be. You can read a verse a day and ponder on all His goodness towards us the rest of the day. Equally you might want to read it all at once and then go back through it at your leisure. Either way the word of God is equivalent to a two-edged sword cutting a swathe through the enemy's lies and deception. The word is alive and active, and as effective today as when it was first written. The word is discerning between the thoughts and intents of our heart bringing them out of hiding, exposing them to our understanding and allowing us to know who we truly are. (Hebrews 4:12)

For we are God's workmanship, created in Christ Jesus to do good works, which God prepared in advance for us to do. (Ephesians 2:10) God created us with a destiny, a purpose that will make a difference in this world. He revels in our discovery of who we really are and what He has placed within us. There is nothing more satisfying than discovering our gifts, talents and destiny and feeling His good pleasure as we exercise them. His word is a light that brings forth the truth of who we are. Let Psalm 91 minister His love for, His desire towards and His pleasure in you.

2 PSALM 91

1 He who dwells in the shelter of the Most High will rest in the shadow of the Almighty.

2 I will say of the LORD, "He is my refuge and my fortress, my God, in whom I trust."

3 Surely he will save you from the fowler's snare and from the deadly pestilence.

4 He will cover you with his feathers, and under his wings you will find refuge; his faithfulness will be your shield and rampart.

5 You will not fear the terror of night, nor the arrow that flies by day,

6 nor the pestilence that stalks in the darkness, nor the plague that destroys at midday.

7 A thousand may fall at your side, ten thousand at

your right hand, but it will not come near you.

8 You will only observe with your eyes and see the punishment of the wicked.

9 If you make the Most High your dwelling-- even the LORD, who is my refuge—

10 then no harm will befall you, no disaster will come near your tent.

11 For he will command his angels concerning you to guard you in all your ways;

12 they will lift you up in their hands, so that you will not strike your foot against a stone.

13 You will tread upon the lion and the cobra; you will trample the great lion and the serpent.

14 "Because he loves me," says the LORD, "I will rescue him; I will protect him, for he acknowledges my name.

15 He will call upon me, and I will answer him; I will be with him in trouble, I will deliver him and honor him.

16 With long life will I satisfy him and show him my salvation."

3 PSALM 91:1

He that dwells in the secret place of the Most High shall abide under the shadow of the Almighty.

I don't know if anyone else has ever thought about this but my mind always asks so where is that? And am I dwelling there?

The Hebrew word 'dwell' has some interesting connotations within it – one of which is to marry, to keep house, to sit down, to settle and remain. The whole idea of marriage and setting up house is interesting as we look at "the secret place". This word secret is to hide or conceal or cover. For the Christian we need to know where our hiding place is.

5

Colossians 3:3 states: "for you died and your life is now hidden with Christ in God." When we accept Jesus Christ as our Lord and Savior He becomes our bridegroom. We get to settle in and setup our home in Christ. He is our bridegroom and the secret place where we are hidden. If we marry Christ, if we make Him our home, then it says that we abide under the shadow of the Almighty. That word abide is to stop over, stay permanently.

So, let's get this straight. When we accept Christ He becomes the secret place – our hiding place – of the most High – God the Father. And because my life is hidden in Christ I now can stay in that place with the Almighty. That name, the Almighty, has a specific revelation. The name God Almighty or El Shaddai in Hebrew was revealed to Abram when God once again told Abram that he would be the Father of many nations – that he would have the son of promise even though his body was old. God wanted to emphasis to Abram that nothing is impossible for Him – He works beyond all circumstances because He is the Lord God Almighty.

Here in Psalm 91 we are reminded that we serve an Almighty God who is in control of every situation and can do and will do what He has promised. That is where we need to set up house and stay permanently – in the shadow of Him who is able to do exceedingly and abundantly above and beyond all we dare think or even ask.

In that shadow we will be kept cool from the heat of the day. In that shadow He is there, a person is never separated from their shadow. Where you go your shadow follows. You are hidden in Christ in God and you have a mighty God that is very close at hand. He will never leave you – He can't because you are dwelling in His secret place. Be confident of this – His name is powerful and you are married to the One whose name is above every name and at His name every knee will bow and no enemy can withstand.

4 PSALM 91:2

I will say of the Lord: He is my refuge and my fortress, my God, in whom I trust.

This is such an interesting verse as it begins with a proclamation or a statement of confession – "I will say!" How important it is for us to confess who God is, what He said He would do and the promises He has for us.

Your words are powerful. Proverbs 18:21 states that your words either bring life or death. That is powerful! Your words today are framing your tomorrows. God said let there be - and there was – out of nothing came forth the creation of our world, the universe, and mankind. The same creative ability rests in your tongue. On the other hand when we speak negatively you cause death – it's a curse. You can prophesy life into dry bones by commanding them to live. Or you can speak out, 'I can't do that and you won't'!

Here in Psalm 91 it says, 'I will say of the Lord'. Why "of the Lord"? That needs to be our focus. It's not about what I can do or can't do; it's about whom He is and what He promised He would do. It's all about our perspective. We can put our eyes on ourselves - our frailty, our limitations and our own resources or we can look to the lord and who He is. We move out of a place of confinement; out of the box. We so often try to live in our own small world, our smallness of mind.

In Joel 3 it says, 'let the weak say I am strong, let the poor say I am rich'. Are you lying? No, you are agreeing with God and who He is in us. Paul says when I am weak then I am strong – how bazaar! It's because greater is He that is in you. If our eyes stay on the Lord and we declare with our mouths who He is, it makes a statement in the heavens. Our mouths release the power of our creator to do what only He can do.

Jesus often spoke to diseases, demons, the wind and waves. He even spoke to the fig tree. In Mark 11:14 He spoke to the fig tree saying: "May no one ever eat fruit from you again" and the following day Peter said, "Rabbi, Look! The fig tree you cursed has withered!" Wow – He spoke to the tree and it died! Notice the word 'cursed'. Jesus didn't swear at the tree, He spoke to it and "endued it with power to fail'. That is what cursed means. Your words have the same power, either for life or death.

Jesus went on in Mark 11 to say, "Have faith in God". That's why you need to - "say of the Lord". We need to remember who He is and what He will do, then speak words of life into being.

5 PSALM 91:3

Surely He will save you from the fowler's snare and from the deadly pestilence.

In verse three the Psalmist is saying 'surely', but surely what? Surely in light of the fact that He is the Almighty and that our trust is in His bigness, He will save us. Surely nothing is too difficult, no problem too small, no mountain too high. Nothing, there is nothing that He won't deliver us from!

It is in this verse that we see we have something trying to trip us up, trap us or ensnare us. This is the enemy of our soul, Satan or the devil. His mandate is three fold: steal, kill and destroy. Peter in I Peter 5:8 calls him your enemy the devil, and Paul says in

Ephesians not to be unaware of the enemy's devices. We are told not to give the enemy a foothold. Jesus said to pray that we are delivered from the evil one. The enemy will bait us like a bird in order to trap us. If you are sick, the enemy will throw thoughts at you about death. What if…? If you are facing a financial difficulty, he will bait you with questions about creditors, poverty, and bankruptcy. If you are embarking on a new job, all the doubts will fly at you that you aren't capable. I Corinthians 10 calls these vain imaginations, arguments that set themselves up against the knowledge of God. We are told to take them captive to the obedience of Jesus Christ. We need to see the bait for what it is – it is spiritual warfare. Our battle is not against flesh and blood but against the enemy. The good news is that God will save you. It is a given! Even though there is a battle we are the victors for our victory comes from the Almighty. There is nothing that is too difficult.

Surely He will save you!

6 PSALM 91:4

He will cover you with His feathers and under His wings you will find refuge; His faithfulness will be your shield and rampart.

What a place of warmth and stillness can be found under the shelter of a wing! Wings are incredible in that they can expand to be inclusive and keep a bird dry in the midst of a storm. I love the saying: "It rolls off him like water off a duck's back".

When we stay under the cover or protection of the Lord our troubles will hit His feathers first and roll off. He has provided a place of security, a safe place under His wing, a place where He pulls us in close to

His heart.

The rest of the verse speaks of His faithfulness. God is faithful – faithful to do what He said He would do. His faithfulness never changes; He is the same yesterday, today and forever. You can rest in the fact that he is the same loving God that apprehended your life, invading it with His kingdom. In fact it says in II Timothy 2:13 that even when we are faithless He remains faithful. That faithfulness is a sure foundation to shield you and keeps you.

Not only is a shield used for protection to ward of arrows or swords from penetrating the holder, a shield also is embossed with the family crest or the coat of arms of the Kingdom. God's faithfulness is like having the Queen's royal signature applied to you. In England, when Her Majesty's crest is found on a product, it means she uses it or endorses it. And so it is with you. The king has His shield around about you because you have His stamp of approval.

Lastly because of His faithfulness to you, you can run into Him and He will keep you. He will be the 'Keep' around you. The rampart or keep was a place of defense in a castle, a place for people to retreat to and be safe in a time of battle. This is the place we run to in our battles. When it looks like the enemy is getting the upper hand and things feel like the arrows are flying over the castle wall, run to your rampart – His faithfulness. That will be your protection, your anchor in the storm. Remember, even when we are faithless, He is still faithful. He never changes: He is the same yesterday, today and forever.

7 PSALM 91:5

You will not fear the terror of the night nor the arrow that flies by day.

I love the fact that this verse directly addresses the night. The night season can be a time of intense spiritual activity. If the children are sick, they always seem worse at night. If you are going through a hard time, your mind seems to be a minefield, particularly at night. I remember one of our children having an ear infection and he cried all night long. The problem was the next day he was fine and we were wrecked.

What is it about the night? The simplest answer is 'darkness'. The enemy works in the dark. The adversary is scheming, plotting and seeking whom he may devour and a 'sudden alarming attack' is what will best bring about his desired results. It is interesting that in our days we have terrorist attacks on innocent people. These are planned so that they bring about fear and destruction. It is the same with the enemy - he wants to bring about a sudden surprise attack so that fear will grip our being.

When would we be most vulnerable? When we are resting, sleeping. But this psalm says we don't have to fear the terror of the night – that we have protection from the scary dreams and visitations in the night. You see our Lord never slumbers nor sleeps – he is always watching over you to keep you from all evil. You are covered with the blood of Jesus Christ. Interestingly before the children of Israel left Egypt the angel of death struck down the first-born sons of the Egyptians but the Israelites were safe if they applied the blood of a lamb on the doorposts. The destruction or the terror of that night could not harm them so they had nothing to fear. And so it is with us as we apprehend the blood of Jesus for our household and ourselves we will not fear the terror of the night.

The arrow that flies by day speaks into that which 'pierces'. The arrows that pierce our hearts the most are the words that are spoken to or over us. The old saying of "sticks and stones may break my bones but names will never hurt me" was most likely made up by someone who encountered the piercing of words. Words do hurt! They have the ability to touch the heart and soul in a way that could plague a person for life. Your words have the power to bring life or death.

Why do they fly by day? Because that is when you are most likely to encounter people! Regardless, we will not fear for in Christ we have the freedom to forgive and break the power of piercing words. They may be flying at us but they cannot poison us, therefore we will **not** fear.

8 PSALM 91:6

Nor the pestilence that stalks in the darkness, nor the plague that destroys at midday.

Growing up in Canada we loved to go camping. It is interesting what can stalk you when it is dark, pitch black, and you are on the way back to your tent from the outhouse. Most of the time the stalking goes on in your mind as you hear the owls hoot or the coyotes howl but its not until you get back in your tent that you meet the pestilence that stalks in the darkness - the mosquito! All it takes is one little mosquito to keep you up all night long, slapping yourself and searching throughout the tent with your flashlight/torch to locate the beast. When you realize what the "pest" is that is stalking your life you can turn the light of the spirit upon it, break its power over you and walk into freedom. The enemy loves to buzz around your head and stalk your mind but when you turn on the light the darkness is gone. Darkness has to flee in the light and we have the light of the world to invite into our darkness so it has to stop the stalking.

The plague of verse 6 is an epidemic – that which brings destruction and ultimately can produce death. We are blessed with many medical breakthroughs and immunization shots for so many diseases. However, it seems like there are still plagues that haunt lives. 'Aids' or 'cancer' are deadly words that can conjure up so much fear. We are promised that we will not fear the plague. Oh, the enemy may come with some symptoms and try to capture and torment your mind or body but it is written: "You WILL NOT FEAR". Psalm 103:3-4 says, "forget not all his benefits – who forgives all your sins and heals all your diseases, who redeems your life from the pit and crowns you with love and compassion, who satisfies your desires with good things so that your youth is renewed like the eagle's". What a benefit package that is – I'd like to see a company try to match that one!

That package is yours and so we need to make a claim

on what is ours. Jesus took all our sin and diseases and "nailed" them so we can be free. Our freedom came at a cost to Him and now we can trust in the fact that 'It is finished'. He took the plague for us at midday so that we can be free all day – every day.

9 PSALM 91:7

A thousand may fall at your side, ten thousand at your right hand, but it will not come near you.

Never underestimate the power of one! David had his mighty men that routed the adversaries over and over. One, Eleazer, son of Dodai, stood his ground when the entire army of Israel retreated. He single-handedly struck down the Philistines till his hand grew tired and froze to his sword. The word goes on to say that the Lord brought about a great victory that day. You see we are called to war but the victory comes from the Lord. So, even if you are the only one fighting the enemy is still defeated. Having done all, stand.

If one can put a thousand to flight and two ten thousand, then you see the power of agreement. Jesus said that if two or more agree as touching any one thing it shall be done for them. The psalm says that ten thousand will fall at your right hand. The right hand signifies power and might. Jesus is sitting at the right hand of the Father – all power and authority are under Him. You have been given that power and might to operate in. If you pick up your sword of the Spirit and allow it to cleave to your hand, you will see the enemy fall away under your right hand.

'It shall not come near you' reminds me of the movie, Lord of the Rings, where Gandalf, staff in hand, empathically says to the dragon, 'YOU SHALL NOT PASS!' And he stood there. This is a picture of what Christ has done for us. He already secured the victory. He triumphed over Satan and took the keys of death and Hades out of his possession. All we do is enforce the victory. Having done all, stand, for it will not come near you.

10 PSALM 91:8

You will only observe with your eyes and see the punishment of the wicked.

In Ephesians 1:18 Paul recites a great prayer that we need to be praying for ourselves. He asks that the eyes of our heart would be enlightened. Why do we need that to happen? It's so we can observe, behold, look intently at with pleasure the work that has been done for us at the cross and ultimately the resurrection of Christ. That we will know the hope to which we were called, the riches of His glorious inheritance that we have as saints and the great power that is available to us who believe!

Yes, we need our eyes open so we can see truth and

know the truth. If we know the truth, it will set us free. We need to know that Jesus is seated at the right hand of the Father and that God has placed ALL things under his feet.

In Ephesians 2:6 it says that God raised us up with Christ and seated us with Him in the heavenly realms in Christ Jesus. From that vantage point we can only observe with our eyes the punishment inflicted on our enemy. Jesus came with a mandate and a purpose; to destroy the works of the evil one (I John 3:8). And that is what He did! He healed the sick, brought recovery of sight to the blind and set the captives free – free from the destruction and harassment of the enemy.

Now from our place of authority we can observe the punishment of the wicked as we pick up our authority and do the works of the Kingdom. We get to go and preach the good news and observe with our eyes wide open the power of God confirming His word with signs following!

11 PSALM 91:9

**If you make the Most High your dwelling
– even the Lord, who is my refuge -**

I like the wording of the King James Bible best for this verse. It states because you <u>made</u> – **not if** you made **but because** you made. There is no condition here. It is saying that He will be your cause. You fight for a cause if you believe in it. Well, the Lord says **you are worth fighting for**. You have a place in Him that is sure and secure.

Most High is a name for God that is first mentioned in Gen. 14:19, 20. In this passage Abram along with 318 men go after the army of four kings that defeated five. These kings took Abram's nephew, Lot, and his possessions and carried him off. When Abram heard, he went after his kin! There was tenacity in his spirit that rose up and said, "No way! You are not having what is mine." And he defeated them and recovered Lot and all his possessions. At this point he meets Melchizedek, King of Salem, and Melchizedek blesses him using God Most High – Jehovah Elyon. This literally means Supreme God or Most Loved God.

In verse 19 of Genesis 14 the God Most High is the possessor of heaven and earth. The earth is the Lord's and all that's in it. All belongs to Him, and was created by Him. So now we praise Him because He is most loved!

In verse 20 Melchizedek says blessed be God Most High who delivered your enemies into your hand. God is the one who fights our battles and delivers the victories. When you think of the odds of 319 men against four kings and their armies, it is astounding! But if God be for us, who can be against us! There is nothing too big for our supreme God. It is He that gives the victory and fights the battles.

Because He, the supreme God, is our dwelling place

we can rest and praise Him who is our victory.

12 PSALM 91:10

Then no harm will befall you, no disaster will come near your tent.

This harm that this verse is referring to is evil. Directly translated it means **to spoil by breaking to pieces** or **to make good for nothing**.

Jesus when He taught His disciples to pray said to pray that we would be delivered from the evil one or from evil. There is one that is behind evil and that is the devil, the accuser of the brethren, the father of lies. If he could he would break you into pieces and render you good for nothing!

However, we have been given a promise that we will be delivered from evil. We have been given authority to overcome. Ephesians 6:11 states that we have been given armor so that we can take our stand against the devil's schemes. Paul clearly states that we aren't in a war with people. There is something higher going on and it involves the spiritual forces of evil in heavenly realms.

Because this is what is happening all about you or above you or for you we need to take hold of the provision of God and put on our armor. How do you go about putting on something that is invisible? It comes from the understanding of what each piece represents, not going through some motions of figuratively putting something on.

A belt is used to hold a garment up so it doesn't fall around your ankles and trip you up. When we know truth, it sets us free from the trap of lies. The enemy is the father of lies and when we believe a lie we are imprisoned. However, when we have revelation of truth, we are set free from the lie. It is important to keep the belt securely notched so we don't get tripped up believing a lie. When we know the truth, we can stand on it like a rock under our feet.

The breastplate of righteousness needs to be in place. Our righteousness is in Jesus Christ. We are the righteousness of God in Christ Jesus. Not because of the great things we do or don't do but because of Him. It is so important to know this as a reality as the enemy will always question your righteousness.

Your feet fitted with a good pair of hiking boots – the readiness that comes from the gospel of peace. The gospel is good news! We have been reconciled with our Father and now we have been given the same ministry: the ministry of reconciliation. Jesus died for us all that we might have a loving relationship through him with the Father. This ministry is one of love. Be ready to share the love of God for God is love.

In addition to this the writer of Ephesians says take up the shield of faith with which you can extinguish all the flaming arrows of the evil one. It is your faith that will quench the flames and break the arrows that are flung at you. Your faith is like a fire extinguisher to the devil's plans. They may come blazing at you but your faith in God Almighty will be a shield about you. With God all things are possible. Mark 11:22 says have faith in God. When we trust Him, He is our shield; our protection and no evil can make us "good for nothing"!

Put salvation on your head as a helmet. Your mind is the battlefield. We constantly need to renew our minds with what that salvation entails: healing, deliverance, wholeness, completeness and eternal life.

The sword of the spirit is the word of God and with it comes the ability to wield it. A sword is of no effect if left in its sheath. But the word is alive and active, sharp and powerful! We need to draw it out letting it flow from our mouths. Jesus said 'it is written' to the devil thereby overcoming him. We too can rest in all the armor that has been provided for us knowing we will be delivered from all evil.

13 PSALM 91:11

For He will command his angels concerning you to guard you in all your ways;

In our western mindset the thought of angels may make you think of fairies like Tinkerbelle of Peter Pan fame. But the bible teaches us in Hebrews 1 that angels are ministering spirits sent to serve those will inherit salvation.

You can see the work of angels through looking at their recorded activities. Jacob saw angels ascending and descending from heaven. Angels come to earth on assignment. This scripture, Psalm 91, says that

God commands them to guard you, protect you, keep you and guide you in all that you do, wherever you go. Ps 34:7 says that they encamp around you and deliver you. In Luke 1 we see the angel Gabriel delivering a message to both Zechariah and Mary. Another angel appears to Joseph with a warning and a message. An angel came and stirred the waters at the pool of Bethesda and released healing.

Angels are not a myth. They are part of the spiritual realm of the Kingdom of God. They are sent to minister or serve you and me.

When we travel we pray for the angels to surround us, protect us and keep us in all our ways. Once my husband had an encounter with a demonized man. He had a grip on Jim, threatening to punch him. Jim just looked at him and said you can't do that because the angel of the Lord encamps around about me to deliver me. As Jim quoted the scripture this man's strength was sapped and he let go. You see the Lord has sent the angels to minister unto us to keep us in all our ways.

I am very convinced that many of us are delivered from serious difficulties because the Lord has sent an angel. Peter was in prison. While the church had gathered to pray for his deliverance Peter has a visitation from an angel who said, "Get up, get dressed and follow me". He leads him right out of the prison opening all the locked gates. Peter thought he was dreaming – that this must be wishful thinking! But God had sent an angel to deliver him and guard him in all his ways. This supernatural deliverance is ours for the word says "He will command them to minister to us, the heirs of salvation!"

14 PSALM 91:12

For they will lift you up in their hands so that you will not strike your feet against a stone.

This picture reminds me of walking with little children. As a parent we can see the path ahead that they can't. If it starts to get uneven, rocky, slippery or dangerous in any way we would pick the little ones up and carry them to the next level to a safe part of the path. The child does not even realize that they have just been delivered from a potential hazard. They just feel the security of a loving parent. This is the ministry the angels provide for you and me. They carry us, protect us, and guard us through potentially dangerous situations in our lives.

I remember one time while we lived in Northern Alberta, Canada my husband's mother had passed away. My husband had flown down to be with her and the other two brothers. The funeral was 1100 miles away and I needed to drive from our town to make the journey. We had four young children and it started to snow very strongly during the night. By morning the newscast said the police were going to close the highway as a blizzard was closing in. They said if you need to get out of town go now! That was my cue. I knew I needed to go. I got all the bags and gear required along with the kids into the car. Then we prayed together for the angels to surround us and keep us. I said to the kids just be quiet and pray. We prayed our way through. The snow was flying, the wind was howling. I remember at one point there were 24 large trucks coming toward me. They create their own swirl of snow so I couldn't see anything but a white blanket of snowflakes. I know beyond a shadow of a doubt that the angels were there to lift us up in their hands. That was the worse car journey of my life but glory goes to the Lord for He sent His angels to protect, keep and deliver us from all evil.

15 PSALM 91:13

You will tread upon the lion and the cobra; you will trample the great lion and the serpent.

Jesus in Luke 10 picks up this scripture. We see him sending 72 out to do the "stuff" – the work of the Kingdom. They come back all excited that even the demons submit in His name. He, then, confirms this back to them by stating He has given them authority! What a word – EXOUSIA in fact! It means delegated influence, power, right, or strength – the word even suggests superhuman.

Jesus has given us all power and the authority to

trample on the works of the enemy. So often we ignore the fact that we have an enemy and that it is our responsibility to use what we have been given. Trample is not just a walk in the park but a stomping with the intent to inflict pain.

We have been told the fields are white and ready to harvest. He didn't say oh by the way you only have a push mower to get the job done! No, he has given us the "John Deer" harvesters to take the fields on. Can you imagine a wheat farmer going into his field with a push mower as opposed to the power of the combine machinery?

Jesus has given us this kind of power over the works of the enemy. We need to pick up our authority and begin to bring the Kingdom of God into the Kingdom of darkness.

The rest of the verse in Luke says that nothing by any means will harm you. You need that assurance that nothing can harm you – you are free from the sting of the scorpion and the bite of the snake - but you need to take your God given right and say no to the enemy. Paul says we are not unaware of the enemy's devices and Peter says resist him. We need to use the authority that we have been given with full assurance that if God be for us who can stand against us. Jesus sent the 72 out to destroy the works of the evil one – we too have been given all power and authority so that we can work the works of God without fear!

Maybe its time that we like superman, Clark Kent, put on the clothes provided for us through the Holy Spirit and do some rescuing of our own. Jesus said you would be clothed with power from on high. Why? So you can go into the entire world and do the works of the Kingdom.

16 PSALM 91:14

"Because he loves me," says the Lord, "I will rescue him; I will protect him, for he acknowledges my name."

Have you ever wondered what we need to do to prove to the Lord that we love Him? It almost seems insignificant to say to Him, "I love you." **But you are not insignificant to Him.** He created you in His own image with the desire for fellowship, communion and relationship with Him.

This verse reveals to us that to show the Lord God Almighty that we love Him all we have to do is acknowledge His name! Amazing! It reminds me of when our own kids were little and they would be playing with a bunch of other tots. If there was one cry or one call of 'Mommy' from one of our children, they immediately had my attention. A parent can distinguish their child's cry from all the others. They know if it means they are hurt, needs the toilet, are whining, or just wants the assurance you are there.

The Father promises that if we set our love on Him, that if we join or cling to Him, because we acknowledge His name that He is there for us. All we have to do is call out His name. Call upon me and I will answer you, ask and it shall be given to you. If you ask the Father anything in my name it shall be done for you. These are the promises we need to know.

When we acknowledge His name we submit ourselves under His mighty hand. Sometimes like a child we just need the assurance of a hug. Even as a grandparent I love it when the kids run up, throw their little arms around me, and say I love you. There is something about being acknowledged and loved.

Our heavenly Father says that simply because we love Him and call on His name He is there for us. He will rescue us from the 'bullies' in our lives and He will protect us. There is nothing like the safety of the caring Father's arms to keep you secure!

17 PSALM 91:15

**He will call upon me, and I will answer
him; I will be with him in trouble, I will
deliver him and honor him.**

In this day with telephones, Internet, mobile phones
and Blackberry you would think that you should have
no problem speaking to people. The problem arises
when the person that needs to respond to the call
doesn't. There are times when my husband says to
me I called you 3 times and you didn't answer.
Where are you? How frustrating!

The good news is that we don't need technology to
get in touch with God. All we have to do is call and

He promises he will answer. You won't even get the answering machine.

In Daniel 3 we read of three young men, Shadrach, Meshach and Abednego. They would not bow to the spirit of the age and ended up in an extremely hot fire. I love what they said to Nebuchadnezzar. We don't need to defend ourselves before you in this matter. If we are thrown into the blazing furnace, the God we serve is able to save us from it and He will rescue us from your hand, O King. Into the fire they went all bound. But God says in this scripture that He will be with us in trouble and with them He was. The King even saw a fourth person in the furnace and all of them were walking about freely.

The King was amazed. He called them out to find that they were unharmed, not a hair singed, robes not scorched and they didn't even smell of fire! Now that is deliverance! But it doesn't end there. It then goes on to say that the King promoted them all. That's honor!

The Lord says call on me for His promise to us is that He hears every cry. Because He hears He will be with us in the fiery trials, He will deliver you from all evil and He will honor you.

18 PSALM 91:16

"With long life will I satisfy him and show him my salvation"

Psalm 91 is a great psalm full of the promises of the Almighty God. In the beginning verse we start with that great name and in that name we remember that nothing is impossible with Him. So long life is not an issue to the author and giver of life.

Both of my husband's parents died at an early age. Heart problems took their toll and their lives. The medical system is always saying this is genetic – you have a 'higher risk' because of your genetic heritage. But we have a higher gene pool running in us in whose blood we trust. Jesus took all our sins, all our disease and nailed them to the tree. His strips have healed us. We need to know that He died and took our sickness and sins that we might be free. Free from all the bad news of death and destruction of the medical system.

With long life will I satisfy him! My grandmother died at 103! She was an amazing woman. She was strong and living on her own up to the end. She was satisfied with long life! Not many would want to live 103 years but the bible does talk about 3 score and 10 or 70 years.

I love what Caleb says in Joshua 14:11. He was 85 years old at this point and he says I am still as strong today as the day Moses sent me out. I am just as vigorous to go out to battle now as I was then; now give me this hill country! Wow! What a confession – I am strong and vigorous and I have ground yet to cover. Lord, help us all to have this attitude at any age.

The Lord wants to show you his salvation. This word, salvation, is not just eternal life although it does include that. It means victory, prosperity, health and deliverance. It is the full meal deal! When you go to McDonalds, (not that anyone ever admits that they eat there) you can order a cheeseburger alone or you can have the meal deal. You then get it all – all the fat and salt you would want in one meal. And so it is with salvation. Jesus has done all for us but we need to embrace the whole 'meal deal'. Why? Because He wants to show us His goodness, His faithfulness, His love and His power and let that flow in and through our lives.

19 CONCLUSION

As you have read there have been many "aha!" moments. Revelation is wonderful. It's God speaking to us. It's personal what each person hears from God. You may excitedly share it with a friend or partner hoping that they too will see what you see. The glazed look in their eyes means they understand the words but don't have the same enlightened moment that you have.

Revelation is wonderful but it begs for something more. Many times we will hear truths that excite us but we let them slip away. The daily grind of life seems intend upon robbing us of the joy of newfound truths.

Revelation requires application to be truly powerful. Ask the Lord to help you apply it to your life. Pray the revelation. Praise Him for His love and His goodness.

Write it down. Don't let it slip away. Let each one become a building stone in the foundations of your faith. Be strengthened in hope, faith and love.

ABOUT THE AUTHOR

Bonnie Inkster is passionate about the presence of the Lord. This passion overflows in her speaking, teaching, writing and leading.

Besides church planting with her husband, Jim, she initiated a prayer ministry in 2003 called Gateways Ministry to intercede for the nations of Europe. She gathered, trained and led teams into more than 30 nations in Europe in the next 5 years. The ministry subsequently expanded to praying for nations throughout the world. Bonnie loves intercession.

She speaks at seminars and conferences worldwide. Bonnie and Jim together conduct seminars on marriage, parenting, leadership and a host of other topics.

Bonnie has been married 41 years, has 4 children and 9 grandchildren.

OTHER BOOKS AND RESOURCES BY JIM AND BONNIE INKSTER

24 Secrets To Great Parenting
(paperback)

Jim and Bonnie share from their vast experience the principles that helped them raise four great children. It is written in a light-hearted, easy reading style perfect for the busy parent with very little spare time on their hands.

Available through Amazon and on Kindle.

8 Questions Every Parent Wants Answered (DVD)

Jim and Bonnie surveyed hundreds of parents to find what issues are their greatest concern regarding their children. Eight questions were consistent from parents throughout the world.

These questions have been addressed in a powerful and entertaining format. Each session takes less than 10 minutes with great ideas for successful application within your family.

Available through Amazon.

OTHER BOOKS AND RESOURCES BY JIM AND BONNIE INKSTER

24 Secrets to Great Parenting
(audiobook)

Jim and Bonnie felt that this great book had to be available to everyone including those who don't like to read. The research shows men prefer to listen, women prefer to read.

Jim was professionally studio recorded reading this charming and helpful book. Great for in the car or on your personal player when exercising or simply chilling.

Great Blogs @ www.jimandbonnie.co.uk

Jim and Bonnie write a weekly blog giving thoughtful and sometimes witty insights into relationships, marriage and parenting.

Don't miss it!

OTHER BOOKS AND RESOURCES BY JIM INKSTER

Eyes of Wonder
(paperback)

Eyes of Wonder is a delightful collection of life experiences with the children and grandchildren that have taught Jim everything he needed to know to be an adult.

Similar to the Chicken Soup for the Soul series this gives you simple downhome wisdom. Always good for a chuckle too!

Available through Amazon and on Kindle.

The Heart of the Matter
(paperback)

The Heart of the Matter is an interesting journey into the heart of God and our response to His amazing unconditional giving. It reveals excellent revelation and insight into the heart of our heavenly Father.

Available through Amazon and Kindle

Great Blogs

www.gatewaysministries.com

www.jimandbonnieinkster.com

Jim and Bonnie can be contacted through these websites.

www.ingramcontent.com/pod-product-compliance
Lightning Source LLC
Chambersburg PA
CBHW031613040426
42452CB00006B/495